ENERGY FIELD SEAL

REJUVENATE, RECHARGE AND RESTORE

Dr. JOANNE FLANAGAN

ARNICA PRESS

DISCLAIMER

The material contained in this book has been written for informational purposes and is not intended as a substitute for medical advice, nor is it intended to diagnose, treat, cure, or prevent disease. The author and the publisher disclaim any liability arising directly or indirectly from the use of this book. If you have a medical issue or illness, consult a qualified physician. The statements in this book have not been evaluated by the united states FDA. Use of this book is at your own risk.

Published by ARNICA PRESS
www.ArnicaPress.com

Written by Joanne Flanagan
Photos form Joanne Flanagan personal archives
Additional photos by Shutterstock

Copyright © 2022 Joanne Flanagan
www.equilibrex.com
www.DrJoanneFlanagan.com

Printed in the United States of America
ISBN: 978-1-955354-32-5

I am the author of my life.
Every chapter has made me realize
that my thoughts create the person that I am.
Gratitude is most important.
Every day unfolds a new step in our journey.
We must live in the present and appreciate every moment!

~ Dr. Joanne Flanagan

ENERGY
FIELD SEAL

REJUVENATE, RECHARGE AND RESTORE

Dr. JOANNE FLANAGAN

Table Of Contents

INTRODUCTION

S everal years have passed since I began writing this book, and researching the energies around us that affect our lives. There is so much continuous new research that I had to stop and evaluate which was pertinent to living a healthy and vibrant long life. I would love to see everyone living a happy, stress-free life with no illnesses or emotional problems.

Keeping yourself in balance is the key to adding life to your years, and years to your life! Everyone can benefit by knowing how to identify the energy draining things around us both physical and mental. We shouldn't ignore all of the new technology that is creating frequencies that disrupt your body's natural functioning abilities. Also all of the new chemicals in the environment and genetically altered foods have an effect on your energy balance. I will point these things out to you so that you can take measures to keep your equilibrium.

Everything in the universe has a frequency – energy, including all biological life as well as the Earth itself. Our bodies are integrated electrical systems that can be influenced by outside frequencies, since every cell communicates and operates by electrical impulses. Once you understand this bio-energy, you can counteract the aging process and damaging frequencies that can destroy your body.

My interest in stress reduction began in middle school, where I encountered many stressful situations in every area of my young life. I tried different strategies and many of them worked to keep me balanced. When I began working on my doctorate degree, I taught post-graduate courses on "Dealing With Stress" at UWM – University of Wisconsin, Milwaukee.

I wrote the book *Secrets Of Revitalization* with my then husband Dr. Patrick Flanagan. We were searching for ways to slow down the aging process and how to add life to your years, and years to your life. We traveled around the world every few months, hoping to find the latest discoveries and research on anti-aging. We did learn a lot.

I also founded SuperBodies®, Inc. which is devoted to researching the many theories and products associated with health and wellness and then doing experiments to see their validity. Since this is directly associated with the aging process, I have spent many years doing this, and am still continuing my research.

While traveling around the world, I found that different shapes and designs had either a strengthening or weakening effect on the body. We had many scientific instruments to measure different energies emitted from different designs. We slept in the Pyramid in Giza and measured its vibrational energy.

I did make a significant discovery – The Equilibrex® Pendant, for which I received a trademark. I tried to duplicate the energy of the Pyramid in Giza in the Equilibrex® Pendant. The design's vibration on both sides of the pendant is what gives it the power to enhance your body's vibration by creating an energy balance. This has been tested for many years.

The experiments with the Equilibrex® Pendant showed that plants that were given treated water with the pendant soaked in the water for thirty minutes, grew significantly faster and larger than the plants just watered with regular water. We also experimented with rubbing the Equilibrex® Pendant on a cigarette, and the cigarette no longer weakened the smoker's body when tested with kinesiology, before and after with the smoker holding the cigarette in his hand.

Hundreds of experiments were done, both on water and on the body. The design keeps the body in balance, which helps to maintain good health and wellness. This will be discussed in a later chapter. In this book I will point out all of the things that have an effect on our bodies, and how we can utilize this information. This will include controlling stress, exercise, sleep, nutrition, and meditation.

Enjoy the journey!

Dr. Joanne

EQUILIBREX ® PENDANT STRESS RELIEF IN THE FORM OF MATHEMATICS AND GEOMETRY

The Equilibrex® Pendant by SuperBodies® is a unique bio-energy enhancer designed to keep you balanced in an unhealthy world. Equilibrex® Pendant strengthens your resistance and resilience to the effects of stress. It increases your energy and enhances your mental clarity and mental performance, especially under pressure.

It strengthens your resistance to electromagnetic pollution electromagnetic fields EMF Z – such as computers, cell phones, and other electronic devices. It supports your mental and physical balance, which is essential for optimal health.

Most people suffer from some form of stress, which can be harmful physically, mentally and emotionally. However, according to the makers of Equilibrex® , stress doesn't have to affect us this way. Equilibrex® is a pendant that is manufactured based on the irrational number of Phi, also referred to as the

Golden Ratio, and helps relieve stress as well as block other forces that can be detrimental to the human body.

Using Phi as its basis, Equilibrex's geometrical structure is a precise reproduction of energy forces often called "Life energy" or "Chi." Using Equilibrex® helps strengthen the user's resistance to the effects of both stress and electromagnetic fields, increases their energy level and improves their mental performance.

The number Phi (1.6180339887) is often encountered when taking the ratios of distances in simple geometric figures. Phi has been found to have applications in architecture, the human body, plants, DNA and more. The use of Phi in the creation of Equilibrex® helps reduce stress and give users more energy. Stress can come in many forms, including newer technologies, work and family life. I wanted to create a product that will strengthen users' resilience to known and hidden stressors in the world today, helping them obtain balance and live a fuller, happier life. Usage of Equilibrex® can vary from user-to-user. You should wear Equilibrex® when you are feeling stressed or unbalanced. Equilibrex® works on an individual basis and will give you the balance you need, nothing more or less.

THE BIOENERGY ENHANCER
— ENERGY OF CHI

We read and hear about stress, and are surrounded by it every day – at home, work, school, and the likes. There are many invisible stressors such as electromagnetic radiation emitting from microwaves, high power electric lines and cell phones, that you may not even be aware of.

THE PROBLEM

Our modern, technological lifestyle has produced damaging effects which are well documented. Our bodies lack balance, we feel uneasy, and mentally or physically drained.

THE SOLUTION

The body is a complex and highly sophisticated organism. It needs to be kept in balance in stress-filled environments. When out of balance, our bodies begin to break down. Our immune systems weaken which increases our vulnerability to a variety of ailments.

The Equilibrex® bioenergy enhancer has been researched and proven to stabilize your energy flow at the molecular level. This powerful effect is due to the geometrical blueprint of Equilibrex® which combines five predominant patterns in nature which relate to forms of energy exchange. This is called life energy or chi.

Equilibrex® is a subtle energy regulator. It is a unique and significant breakthrough in maintaining balance in and around the body. When worn around the neck, you are capable of improving mental focus, balance, response to stress, and increase your overall energy level.

THE RESULTS

How much better you feel and how much energy you have, depends on how far out of balance you actually are. The more imbalanced the energy field, the longer it will take for you to reach a state of equilibrium.

Most people feel some effects right away. They report a sense of calmness, a feeling of well-being, improved sleep, better mental focus, less fatigue, absence of discomfort, and more energy.

World class athletes report that the Equilibrex® Pendant improves their mental focus and gives them a significant competitive edge. Advanced clinical studies conducted at VibraLife Institute have shown that the use of Equilibrex® can reduce your stress levels up to 75% over a period of 30 days. Individual results may vary.

INSTRUCTIONS — HOW TO USE

Wear the Equilibrex® Pendant around your neck either under or over your clothes. The effect is still the same.

Wear the back – which has SuperBodies® engraved in it – next to your body.

We do not recommend sharing the Equilibrex® bioenergy enhancer, as everyone's energy field is different, and the underlying geometrical structure of the Equilibrex® needs to configure itself to one energy field to be most efficient.

CAUSES OF STRESS

We read about it, hear about it, complain about it, and are constantly surrounded by it. It permeates every area of our life, regardless of age, background, socioeconomic status, or gender.

Stress occurs when the pressure upon us exceeds our threshold to cope with those pressures. Stress is the result of how your mind and body react when confronted with demanding situations. Stress may result from anything that interferes with the smooth and efficient operation of your cells, and throws you out of balance. The event that triggers this reaction may be termed a stressor. It's a fact of life that you are continuously encountering such stressors, some of which you may not even be aware of.

WHAT CAUSES STRESS? Stress emanates from both external and internal factors. The major causes of stress can be divided into three broad categories: Physical/environmental, Social, and Psychological. Everyone has his individual way of expressing stress. I'm sure each and everyone of you has experienced its bad effects: the knotted stomach, headaches, increased heartbeat, sweaty palms, nervous habits, neck and back pain, insomnia, anxiety, impatience, anger, irritability, loss of sexual desire, lack of energy – these are just a few symptoms many of you have accepted as simply getting through the day.

PHYSICAL & ENVIRONMENT

- EMF'S

- Noise

- Air Quality

- Water Quality

- Chemical Pollution

- Illness

- Body Injury

SOCIAL & EMOTIONAL

- Poverty

- Unemployment

- Discrimination

- Monotony

- Life Changes/Divorce/Death

- Holidays

PSYCHOLOGICAL

- Anxiety

- Depression

- Guilt

- Worry

- Religion

- Politics

- Relationship Problems

- Interpersonal friction with co-workers

- Friends & Family members

- Economic dislocations

- Feelings of helplessness in the face of national and international events

- Increasing changes in technological innovation

Maintaining a balanced mind and body is the key to good health and happiness. You must be able to recognize the many forms of stress that affect you, and learn to cope with them.

ELECTROMAGNETIC POLLUTION

HIDDEN STRESS HAZARDS IN YOUR HOUSE

Did you know that electromagnetic frequencies (EMF's) above the Environmental Protection Agency's safe limit are assaulting your brainwaves and body every day? Our natural state of wellness is being clouded with electromagnetic waves of invisible radiation – powerful enough to blast wireless communication data through concrete walls and buildings. Imagine how easily it travels through us, especially newborns and young children. We can't see the smog of electro-pollution, but it is affecting us.

Harmful EMF fields are produced by cell phone towers, microwave beams, high power lines, cell phones, televisions, computers, florescent lights, Wi-Fi, hair dryers, cordless phones, video games ,baby monitors, PDA's, hybrid electric cars, and other electrical equipment.

We need to be aware of the biological effects of these hidden stressors – sleeplessness, headaches, dizziness, immune system suppression, electro-sensitivity, "unexplained" cardiac symptoms, decreased fertility, as well as increased risk of brain cancer and neurological disorders.

Many people report having less energy, constant fatigue, and getting sick often. Depression and moodiness are also common symptoms.

While so much research is being done, we need to identify what hazardous things are in our environment, and how to make it safer for our health.

STRENGTHEN YOURSELF
AGAINST EMF'S

* Use a land line whenever possible

* Use a low SAR (Specific Absorption Rate) cell phone. This is the measure of the rate of RF (radio frequency) energy absorption by the body. These cell phone SAR's are available. Use the speaker function rather than putting a cell phone up to your ear.

* Keep cell phone powered off whenever possible.

* Carry cell phone away from your body, with the keypad or front of the phone facing toward the body, and the back or antenna side facing away from the body.

* Use your phone outside of a car, train, elevator, airplane or other confined metal space.

* Use a computer with wired internet access, with the wireless function disabled, to surf the internet,

watch movies, download music, etc., not a mobile phone.

- Keep cell phones, electric alarm clocks, electric lamps, and everything else electric away from your head and sleep zone – at least four feet away.

- NEVER sleep with cell phone powered on. Charge it four feet away from people and pets.

- Replace old electronics, fluorescent lights, and dimmer switches.

- Stay at least three feet from household appliances, such as coffee makers, microwave ovens, toasters, televisions, computers, electric clocks, plugs in walls, electric tools, etc. Unplug appliances when not in use.

A Test To See
How Electromagnetic
Radiation Affects Us

A pplied kinesiology can be used to test EMR's effects on our bodies.

It takes two people, the "tester" and the "subject." This can be viewed on my website at www.equilibrex.com

1. Have the subject stand erect, right arm relaxed at his side, left arm held out straight, parallel to the floor, elbow straight and thumb pointed down toward the floor.

2. Tester will face your subject and place your left hand on his right shoulder to steady him. Then place your right hand on the subject's extended left arm, just above the wrist.

3. Tell the subject to RESIST when you try to push his arm down.

4. Now push down on his arm fairly quickly, firmly, and evenly. The idea is to push hard enough to test the spring and bounce in the arm, not so hard that the muscle becomes fatigued. It is not a question of who is stronger, but of whether the muscle can resist the push and arm stay straight.

By doing this experiment on a subject who is using a cell phone, you'll find that the subject cannot hold his arm up because the radiation is draining his energy in that muscle. This can also test the negative effects of hair dryers and other electrical devices on the body.

For many years, I have researched ways to counteract the energy draining effects of different types of stress and electrical frequencies on the bio-energy field surrounding the human body. By placing the Equilibrex® Pendant in the subject's hand while holding a cell phone or other electrical device, the subject could resist the push and keep his arm strong. This lessens the effects of stress at the cellular level of the human body.

EVERYONE HAS THEIR WAY
OF EXPRESSING STRESS

I'm sure each and everyone of you has experienced some of the symptoms. The symptoms fall into three categories: emotional, physical, and behavioral.

Symptoms are:

- headaches

- knotted stomach, indigestion, gas pain, diarrhea

- changes in appetite

- increased heartbeat

- difficulty breathing

- sweaty palms

- muscular tension

- backaches

- hypertension

- nervous habits

- sleep disorders, insomnia, nightmares

- grinding teeth

- allergies

- decreased enjoyment of sex

- anxiety

- constant worrying

- irritability and anger

- impatience

- apathy (lack of interest, energy, or motivation)

- mental or physical exhaustion

- frequent illness (colds, infections)

- hives or skin rashes

- ears ringing

- feeling faint or dizzy

- procrastination

- Boredom

- forgetfulness

- feeling like crying

- over reacting to situations

- feeling like a balloon about to pop

In today's fast-paced world we experience more stress at every stage of our lives than ever before. We must prevent the symptoms by knowing the causes. The inner devitalizing effects of stress are taking the terrible toll on your physical and emotional health.

- 43% of adults suffer adverse health effects from stress
- 75-90% of all physician office visits have stress related components according to the American psychological Association.

Stress-related conditions that are most likely to produce negative physical effects include:
- An accumulation of stressful situations, particularly those that a person cannot easily control. For example, high pressure work plus an unhappy relationship.
- Persistent stress following a severe acute response to a traumatic event, such as a car accident.
- Inefficient or insufficient relaxation technique
- Acute stress in people with serious illness, such as heart disease

Psychological effects of stress

Studies suggest that the inability to adapt to stress is associated to the onset of depression or anxiety. In one study, two-thirds of subjects who experienced a stressful situation had nearly six times the risk of developing depression with in that month. Some evidence suggests that repeated release of stress hormone produces hyperactivity in the hypothalamus-pituitary-adrenal axis and disrupt normal levels of serotonin, the nerve chemical that is critical for feelings of well-being. Certainly, a more obvious level, stress diminishes the quality of life by reducing feelings of pleasure and accomplishment, and relationships are often threatened.

Your Stress Induced Illness Potential

If any of the following life changes have happened to you recently, circle the corresponding number under the VALUE column. I have numbered the changes on the left under RANK in the order I think of their stress impact.

RANK	EVENT	VALUE
1.	Death of a Spouse or Child	100
2.	Divorce	75
3.	Marital Separation	65
4.	Jail Sentence	63
5.	Death of Close Family Member	63
6.	Personal Injury or Illness	63
7.	Marriage	60
8.	Fired From Work	60

25.	Change in Sleeping Habits	25
26.	Change in Recreational Habits	20
27.	Change in Social Activities	20
28.	Change in Eating Habits	20
29.	Vacation	20
30.	Christmas Season	20
31.	Minor Violations of the Law	20

Total your VALUE score. If it is less than 150, many stress experts believe you only have a small chance of illness in the next year. If it is between 150 and 300, you may have a 50% chance of getting a stress related illness. If your score is over 300, you need to take precautions, such as meditation and exercise to lower your stress level.

Here are actions you can take to improve stressful situations:

• Take a second look at the meaning you assign to an experience. You can convert distress to positive stress just by changing your thoughts about it.

- Talk it out

- Take one thing at a time. Focus only on what you are doing now. Don't look back or ahead too often or too long.

- Don't try to be perfect in everything you do.

- Learn to accept what you can not change.

- Never feel closed in. There are always options for anything you have to do.

- Face problems as they occur, not before it happens.

- Learn to say NO

- Don't expect things

- LOVE YOURSELF

Aging

A ging is generally associated with various decreases in bodily functions as we progress from birth to death. It is a slow but continuous process of growing old.

Our physical and mental capacities become more and more limited. Among the various symptoms of aging, many of us experience a decrease in the elasticity of the skin, hardening of the arteries, reduction of vital lung capacity, an increase in systolic blood pressure, a reduction in hearing sensitivity and visual acuity.

Stress may be the number one accelerator of the aging process.

STRESS AND NUTRITION

S tress looms everywhere and is both inescapable and indispensable in one's life. Stress comes from anything that interferes with the smooth and efficient operation of your cells. Stimuli that produce stress are called stressors and vary in intensity, duration, and nature. Stressors can be physiological, psychological, environmental, nutritional or a combination of any of these.

There are two types o stress that confront people: positive stress (eustress) and negative stress (distress). The first type motivates and stimulates creativity. Distress, however, is destructive to the body, and if prolonged, can lead to physical deterioration. Distress is what everyone is concerned with. Finding ways to lessen the effects of that stress is essential. Nutrition may hold the key!

You must keep in mind that a predisposition to develop stress-related disorders depends greatly on genetic and constitutional factors, past medical history, lifestyle, and habits. Stress response is very individual. What may feel good to one person may cause stress to another. It is how one responds to the situation.

A complex relationship exists between nutrition and stress because stress affects nutrition and nutrition affects stress. Both nutrition and stress are involved in metabolism, neuroendocrine functions, immune functions and peak performance.

The nutritional solution to stress takes more than just sufficient protein and calories. Here is an explanation. Stress triggers three significant stages or reactions. The first of these stages is the alarm stage. Your body prepares for what it perceives as danger, whether it be real or imaginary. Just thinking about a stressful situation, with its ensuing worry and anxiety, is the same as if the real stress condition had actually occurred.

Preparation by your body to meet stress begins with metabolic changes. There is an increased cellular uptake of amino acids. Proteins are broken down to form necessary sugar for immediate energy. The blood sugar level increases. If more sugar is needed to maintain a high blood sugar level when stress is longstanding, the adrenals trigger the liver to release sugar that had been stored there, in the form of glycogen for just such an emergency.

Glycogen converts to glucose in an instant when necessary. When that happens, blood pressure increases, calcium and magnesium are drawn from the bone reserves (which is under the control of the adrenals) and an abnormal amount of sodium is retained. This explains the reason for most cases of uncomplicated high blood pressure – a hyperfunctioning of the adrenals.

The second stage of reaction is called the resistance stage, which is the stage from which your body will rebuild itself by using nutrients supplied by your diet and supplementation. If your diet is inadequate and cannot meet the demands of the stress encountered, your body will try to repair to the best of its ability by robbing nutrients from vital reserve areas until it has exhausted them.

As the stress is brought under control, increased stimulation of the neuroendocrine system abates, tissue repair takes place and normal functioning returns (recovery). If your body stays in a chronic resistance stage of stress, exhaustion will occur.

The exhaustion stage is the third stage of reaction to stress. This is the point of which the raw materials for repair are not being supplied by your diet in adequate amounts and your body reserves are insufficient to meet the needs to rebuild. The majority of illnesses will develop during this stage when repair can no longer take place. This is why your immune system should be strong.

It is the small stresses, day after day, week after week, that are continuously repeated until the body is constantly living in either the alarm or resistance stage 24 hours a day.

Since everyone has uniquely individual nutritional needs, you must experiment to find what works best for you. You should keep a diary of your meals and supplements (include the times, amounts, and types of food ingested, as well as a statement indicating how you feel) on a daily basis. The variables in your log can be adjusted, as well as the types of foods you are adding or deleting.

The stress response places a high demand on certain vitamins and minerals. A carefully chosen diet along with a good supplementation program can enhance your ability to manage stress

Vitamins assist the chemical changes that take place in your body. Minerals (such as iron and calcium) help the vitamins as do protein and amino acids. This collection of vitamins, minerals and protein makes up the enzyme system. Enzymes make possible the chemical changes.

You should talk to a health professional who could assess your needs.

A possible suggested balance of recommended anti-stress nutrients is:

- Amino acid free-form complex capsules

- Protein powder with Octacosanol

- A daily multiple vitamin and mineral supplement that includes copper, chromium, and selenium

- Minerals

Since all of the above mentioned nutrients are interrelated, you must include foods that contain them. Research has shown that extra amounts of calcium, Vitamins B, C, and E, can also boost the immune system.

FOODS TO BEAT STRESS

- Dark Chocolate

- Avocado

- Granola (or other Carbs), eating something high in carbs will prompt your brain to start making serotonin.

- Nuts and Seeds

- Salmon

- Citrus Fruits and Strawberries contain Vitamin C, which helps fight stress. Studies have found that high levels of Vitamin C may ease stress levels.

VITAMINS THAT HELP WITH STRESS

- B-complex

- Vitamin E

- Vitamin C

- Vitamin D

- GABA (Gamma - Aminobulyric Acid), a neurotransmitter, a chemical messenger in your brain.

- Amino Acids

- Always consult a health provider for correct intake and dosages.

DRINKS TO RELIEVE STRESS

- Water (at least 8 glasses a day)

- Lemon Water or Tea

- Chamomile Tea

- Warm Milk

- Tart Cherry Juice

- Kava Tea

- Green Tea

Foods That Help Reduce Anxiety

- Fatty Fish such as salmon, mackerel, sardines, trout, and herring are high in Omega-3's

- Eggs and Egg Yolks are good sources of Vitamin D

- Pumpkin Seeds

- Dark Chocolate

- Chamomile

- Turmeric

- Yogurt

- Green Tea

Biorhythm & Our Lives

We all experience days when we wake up in the morning feeling full of energy and excited about what we are going to be doing this wonderful day to reach the goals we have planned for ourselves. We look good, feel excellent, and our thoughts are very positive about everything around us. We feel that nothing can prevent us from achieving everything we want to accomplish concerning work, school, family, relationships, exercising, etc. Then suddenly, a few days later, even though we have been doing everything exactly the same way, eating the same, sleeping the same, and being around the same environment, for no apparent reason something just isn't right. We have little or no energy, feel weak, can't concentrate, feel irritable, look bad, and so on. Some feel this more than others. "What is happening?" we may wonder.

One explanation for these ups and downs of life comes from an area of study called biorhythm, which concerns the behavioral science of life-energy rhythms. There are many rhythms familiar to each of us. The night/day rhythms (24 hours); the seasonal rhythms (spring, summer, fall, winter); the annual rhythms (365.25 days per year); the rhythms of the moon (29.5 days) – these and many others affect each of us differently.

Within the past century, it has been scientifically proven that we have three energy cycles, or biorhythms. These three biorhythms begin in the positive phase at the moment of birth and continue regularly thereafter until death. The three cycles are: the physical, which lasts 23 days, the emotional – sensitivity, which lasts 28 days, and the intellectual – mental which lasts 33 days. There is no bad news with biorhythms, only information.

The first 11.5 days of the physical biorhythm cycle are considered to be the positive half. During this high period, we give off a lot of energy that peaks around the sixth day from the start of the cycle. At this point we are stronger, can work out the hardest and have more endurance than during the rest of the cycle. We are also more resistant to disease, better coordinated and generally in better physical condition.

During the second 11.5 days of the physical cycle, sometimes called the negative half, the body recharges so that energy can accumulate. This means that we tire more easily, need more rest, and find it hard to exercise vigorously. During this time we are more likely to experience a physical slump, since we are weaker and more vulnerable to disease. The body begins gathering strength for a return to the " high" side of the cycle. If we are in good physical condition, no mishaps or illnesses should occur – we merely experience a reduction in physical energy. It is only during the critical days of the cycle, when the rhythm is changing from positive to negative, or vice versa, that our physical rhythm becomes erratic and unstable that extra caution becomes necessary.

The 28-day emotional sensitivity cycle controls the nervous system and affects disposition, mood, and coordination. During the first 14 days, the positive phase, we are inclined to react in positive and constructive ways to most events. Since we get along better with others and with ourselves during this phase, this first half of the emotional cycle proves to be the best time for undertaking projects that require cooperation, a positive attitude and creativity. This period is great for socializing.

Because the emotional cycle is a powerful and pervasive one, it can modify both the physical and the intellectual cycles more than you might expect. In a period of physical decline combined with an emotional peak, your performance may be great, simply because of the very positive attitude generated by the apex of the emotional phase.

The strengths of the emotional rhythm's influence are also apparent in intellectual and creative endeavors. It is reasonable to think that during the negative part of the intellectual cycle it will be difficult to achieve any major insights or to produce viable ideas. However, if that same period is one of an emotional high, the ideas and insights may flow in a virtual tidal wave. Interestingly, the emotional rhythm is the easiest to track, since each of us is a good judge of our own feelings. Even skeptics about biorhythm admit to an awareness of regular fluctuations in their emotions.

In its 14-day negative phase, the emotional rhythm can create very dangerous results, since feelings affect judgment. The days during which we recharge our emotional powers are poor ones for performing dangerous jobs. Critical emotional days carry much more danger than the days of the negative phase. They leave us open to self-inflicted harm. An emotionally critical day, particularly when it is combined with a critical day in either the physical or emotional cycle, definitely calls for taking all available precautions.

The final phase, the intellectual – mental cycle, originates in the brain and takes 33 days to complete. It affects intelligence, reasoning and comprehension powers. The first 16.5 days, or the positive phase, is a good time for self-improvement through reading and education, since our minds are more open, retentive, and our understanding is at its best. On the other hand, during the negative, or low phase, most of us find it harder to concentrate or think things through with maximum clarity.

When we are in the center of a biorhythm cycle, be it up or down, we undergo a spin period, a phase that may be just as serious as a critical period.

The relative strength of the physical, emotional, and intellectual biorhythms varies among individuals. It is foolish to generalize about which rhythms in which phases will dominate other rhythms and phases, and the problem complicates the question of interpreting mixed days. Heredity and talent help explain these differences. What we are as a result of inherited characteristics will strengthen one or another of our biorhythms; and what we do because of our talents will affect our life. The individual ways that we have developed to deal with the stress of biorhythms also modify the effects of those biorhythms.

To find out to what degree your personal biorhythms affect you, I would suggest the following: Keep a diary for one month. Record your feelings, physical strength, and endurance, ability to concentrate , positive or negative attitude, how you are performing your daily tasks, and other observations about yourself. You may then have a personal biorhythm chart done for you, and compare your findings. You will be surprised!

Biorhythm is a means for you to have a sense of predictability and control over your life in general.

Studies I have seen from all over the world have impressed me as well as many other doctors. Biorhythm is as controversial as supplement use. Regardless, the most recent research indicates a number of findings. First, more calories are burned when individuals are in the positive (up) position of the physical cycle, which suggests that diet conscious individuals should cut caloric intake during the negative (down) phase. Second, most sports injuries occur on biorhythmic "critical" or "mini-critical" days. Third, from an accident prevention viewpoint, it is better to be in a negative physical cycle and not a critical or mini-critical cycle.

Critical Days are when the biorhythms are shifting from high to low cycles, and crossing the line.

Mini-Critical Days are in between the high point of a cycle, and the middle crossing.

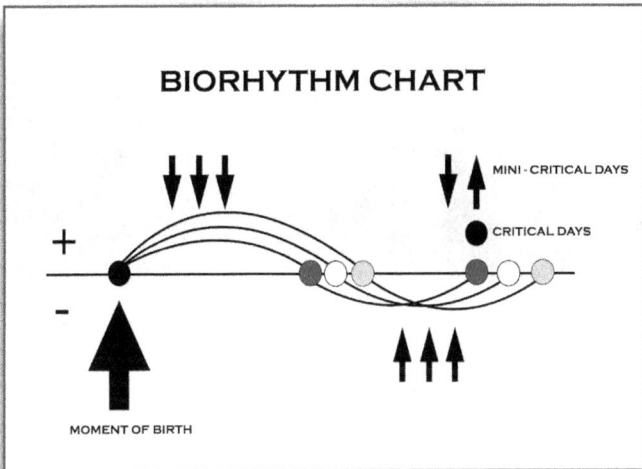

BIORHYTHM CHART

MINI - CRITICAL DAYS

CRITICAL DAYS

+

−

MOMENT OF BIRTH

WHAT IS YOUR RHYTHM?

O ur lives are governed by the clock. We eat, sleep, exercise, work, play, and do everything else according to a time schedule imposed on us by our environment, family, friends, hours that stores are open, etc. For most of us, such strict adherence to the time of the day may create an incredible amount of stress, and drain our energy.

Each individual's energy peaks occur at different times. Everyone knows a "morning person"– someone who wakes up cheery and very energetic. Everyone also knows an "evening person" – someone who can hardly get out of bed in the morning and tend to be sluggish for the first several hours of the day. For both morning and evening people the tables turn late in the evening: Morning people can barely keep their eyes open, while evening people are full of energy.

Whether you are a morning person or an evening person is determined by your internal biological clock, called your circadian rhythm. These rhythms derive from a complex system of internal pacemakers that regulate the timing of hundreds of biological behaviors and processes, including the sleep/wake cycle, growth, cell division, strength, moods, and actions. They also affect our susceptibility to stress and illness. The scientific study of these biological rhythms is called chronobiology. Just wearing an Equilibrex® Pendant, or having it in your pocket, will increase your resistance to stress.

To become aware of your individual rhythms, answer these questions:

- Are you a day or night person?

- Do you have more energy at a particular time of the day?

- Does food taste better later in the day?

- Do you feel an energy drain in the early afternoon?

- Do you think and remember things better at a certain time of the day?

- Do you feel more productive at a particular time of day, regardless of the tasks you are performing?

- Does your sex drive feel stronger at a certain time of day?

If you answered yes to any of these questions, you have an awareness of your biological rhythms. By mastering these rhythms, you can reach your daily potential with less stress and achieve peak performance.

Approximately 20% of the population fall into either "extreme" category. Most people are either moderate morning or evening types, while others are neutral in relation to their circadian rhythms, (from Latin circa dias, "about a day"). This biological clock is characterized by the 24 hour day.

Scientists have discovered that each of us have distinct biological rhythms programmed into our genes. Unfortunately, there is little one can do to change some of the physiological aspects of this. Circadian rhythms behave like an oscillator, causing daily fluctuations, with each cycle lasting for different amounts of time. Adjust your physical and mental limits according to how you feel. Schedule the most challenging tasks for times when you have the most energy.

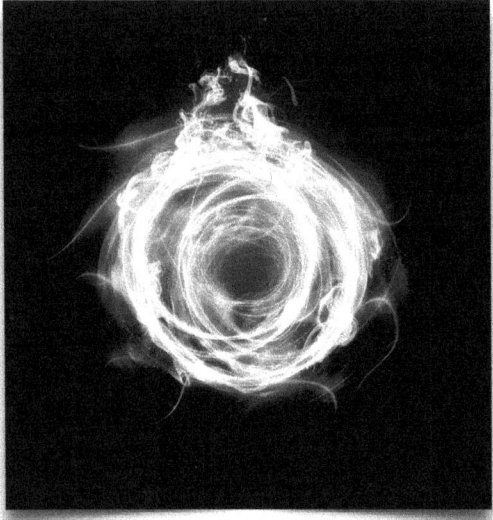

TRIPLE YOUR ENERGY

Vibralife Institute Laboratories are proud to introduce Equilibrex®, the only scientifically proven "Energy Field Regulator" in existence today that does not require any man made external source of power.

Equilibrex® was designed in laboratories with the highest degree of precision to duplicate the geometrical structure of the manifestations of higher energies constituting what is commonly known as life force. It acts as a constant pulse transmitter that generates a powerful energy field similar to the one created by the forces responsible for our vital energy. This process neutralizes potentially harmful molecular vibrations by magnifying stable energy fields.

The key to Equilibrex's success lies in its mathematical blueprint. Equilibrex's design is a mathematical reproduction of the Universal Life Force geometrical configuration. Its Quandra-dimensional design acts as a transformer that intensifies ascending energies by magnifying specific frequencies. It was designed by physicists on the Phi mathematical ratio. Everything in nature contains this ratio.

Introduce Equilibrex® to any living system, and the result is a more powerful, well-balanced, and extremely healthy energy field. We all know the vital importance of a strong energy field. Modern science is now just recognizing its mere existence. A strong and balanced energy field leads to a healthy physical life, but more importantly, it insures that we are mentally ready to tackle all of our daily problems and exponentially better our lives.

We have discovered that when Equilibrex® is introduced to a living system, its entire structure rearranges itself at the molecular level to become more ordered, and closer to the structure of a purer element. In fact, extensive studies have shown that contaminated aqueous solutions rapidly transform and show amazing signs of purification within a very short amount of time. When the Equilibrex® Pendant is worn anywhere on the body, the living system becomes balanced, and enjoys vital energy. Combine this with meditation, proper nutrition, exercise, and positive thoughts, your energy will definitely triple!!!

REgain Control Of Your Life

The Equilibrex® Pendant is the only scientifically proven "Energy field regulator" in existence today that does not require any man made external source of power.

Equilibrex® was designed in a laboratory with the highest degree of precision to duplicate the geometrical structure of higher energies constituting what is commonly known as life force. It acts as a constant pulse transmitter that generates a powerful energy field similar to the one created by our vital electrical energy. This process neutralizes potentially harmful molecular vibrations by magnifying stable energy fields.

Our bodies run on electricity. Electrical signals between your neurons carry messages to your brain. Your heart, muscles, and organs all run on electricity, too. An electroencephalogram (EEG) measures the voltage and records the electrical activity of our brain, and when that last spark of electricity is zero, we are dead.

Introduce Equilibrex® to any living system and the result is a more powerful, well-balanced and extremely strong energy field. This can be tested with kinesiology and scientific meters.

Equilibrex® has conclusively demonstrated under rigorous testing that it changes the molecular configuration of water. Since the average human body is 70% water, there is a profound balancing effect on our energy. Utilizing Dr. Masaru Emoto's experiments on the study of crystalline structures, we put Equilibrex® into several aqueous environments. We discovered fascinating facts on the effect of Equilibrex® in balancing water.

• Equilibrex® manifests enough energy to purify and balance biological systems.

• Equilibrex® reproduces vibrations capable of balancing emotions and blocking the effects of stressors.

• Equilibrex® acts as a protective shield against disruptive Electromagnetic fields (Cell phones, computers, wi-fi, TV, microwave ovens, etc)

THE EXPERIMENTS

We obtained several samples of water from different sources for our experiments. The samples were then exposed to cigarette smoke, an Electromagnetic field (EMF), an argument, and pollution.

The samples were frozen at -25C (-13F) and taken out to observe at -5C (41F) under a digital microscope at magnification of X200.

Photos were taken. After the initial observations, we introduced the Equilibrex® into the samples of water for various periods of time and refroze the samples with the same temperature as before. We then took them out to observe the crystalline structures of those identical samples. Photos were taken.

THE RESULTS

E quilibrex®   rearranged the molecular structure of   ALL of the samples studied, reversing the effects of pollution, electromagnetic fields, and different stressors. It generated a vibration strong enough to restructure the water molecules to their purest and most efficient configurations.

Since the human body is 70% water, we are excited about the positive effects it has on us!

PLANTS WATERED WITH
AND WITHOUT EQUILIBREX

WITH EQUILIBREX   WITHOUT EQUILIBREX

POLLUTED WATER FROM MILWAUKEE RIVER

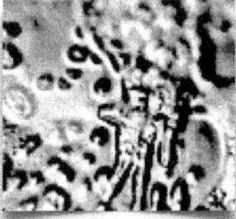

WITH EQUILIBREX

WATER EXPOSED TO A HEATED ARGUMENT

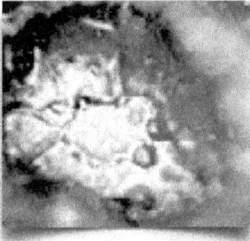

WITH EQUILIBREX

WATER EXPOSED TO LIGHT EMF

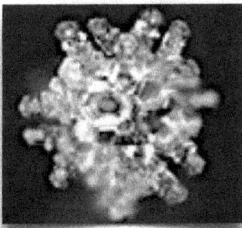

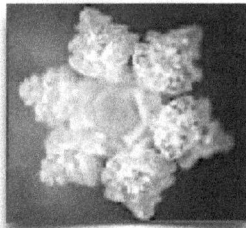

WITH EQUILIBREX

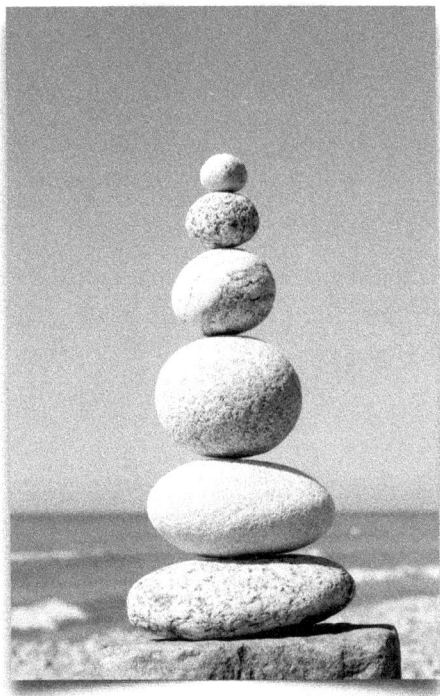

INCREASE YOUR MENTAL FOCUS

Modern scientists have come to realize what has been known for centuries: Everything in our universe is vibrating! Molecular vibration is the fuel of existence, and all vibrations have corresponding geometrical manifestations.

It is a well known fact that sound can be measured in frequencies. All sounds manifest a specific geometric structure that is unique to each individual sound only. Our latest research has proven that thoughts also have specific frequencies plus geometrical patterns and the very same is true for all forms of energy. The EEG (electroencephalogram) measures different frequencies within the brain. A frequency is the number of times a wave repeats itself. Thoughts are energy signals that are transmitted. In order to increase your mental focus level and reduce the effects of stress, one must raise mental vibrations.

Equilibrex® precisely reproduces the geometric patterns of five key elements of existence, which we call Life Energy, evolution, proportion, unity, direction, and purpose. The geometric representation of these elements dictates a duplication of those forces, like a shadow demands a presence and vice versa.

Equilibrex® not only continuously attracts higher vibrations, but it concentrates those forces into one field, becoming a second source of life energy.

The vibrational field generated by Equilibrex® interacts with the one generated by your body. The process produces a state of equilibrium. Certain emotions and thought patterns, such as joy, peace, and acceptance, create higher frequency vibrations, while other feelings and mindsets, (such as anger, despair, fear) vibrate at a lower rate. Pertaining to the Laws of Physics, the Equilibrex® vibrations are higher in energy than yours, (transferring that energy to you), to help counteract the lower vibrations around you. This process will reduce the effects of stress and increase your mental focus potential until a balances state is reached.

Equilibrex® provides you with a source of power that helps defer the harmful, unhealthy vibrations in your daily life (both mental and environmental). It acts as an energy field purifier that constantly elevates your physical performance and increases your mental focus.

EMOTIONS CAN MAKE
A DIFFERENCE IN
YOUR ENERGY BALANCE

We have shown with numerous tests on water how emotions can affect your body, since your body is made up of mostly water. This in turn has an effect on your energy level and balance. I have found that by wearing the Equilibrex® Pendant and holding it in my hands, my energy stays balanced and I remain calmer than without it.

Emotions occur in response to some kind of stimulus (actual, imagined, or past) such as:

• A physical event

• A social encounter

• Remembering or imagining an encounter

• Thinking about, talking about, or reenacting a past emotional experience

Emotions prepare us to deal with events, without having to think about them. We don't choose to feel them, they just happen to us automatically.

An emotional reaction varies from person to person based on their unique personal experiences. Even though we can't choose the emotions we feel, we can choose the ways in which we respond to them.

Humans have up to 27 different emotions, but I identified only six as basic emotions.

- Anger

- Happiness/Joy

- Fear/Surprise

- Sadness

- Worry

- Disgust

How we feel psychologically has an effect on us physiologically. There is a definite link between our minds and bodies. Having an imbalance in any of our organs can lead to health issues.

Eight ORgans Connected To Our Emotions

1. Heart

The heart is the principal organ of the body, and the emotion associated with it is joy, love, or excitement. If there is excessive joy or overexcitement, it can lead to an imbalance, causing insomnia, nightmares, restlessness, mania, and palpitations.

2. Liver

The liver's primary functions are to produce bile, break down nutrients, excrete hormones, and store glycogen. Too much anger leads to resentment, jealousy, irritability, rage, and hatred which causes the production of too much bile.

Symptoms of liver imbalance include dizziness, blurry vision, headache, stiff neck, and hypertension.

3. Spleen

The emotion associated with the spleen is worry or anxiety. Scientifically, the spleen stores blood and produces white blood cells for enhanced immunity.

Symptoms of spleen imbalance include depression or exhaustion. Some people lose their appetite, and have digestive issues.

4. Kidneys

Fear is associated with the adrenal glands and kidneys. The kidneys are responsible for flushing out toxins from the body.

Symptoms of kidney imbalance are hot flashes, night sweats, and frequent urination.

5. Lungs

The lungs are second in line as the body's principal organs. Sadness and grief are associated with these organs.

Too much grief and sadness can lead to shortness of breath, chest tightness, asthma, eczema, and frequent crying.

6. STOMACH

The emotions affecting the stomach (or gut) include nervousness, fear, and sometimes rage. People may have " butterflies in their stomach" before public speaking or in nervous situations.

Excess negative emotions in an imbalanced stomach can lead to choleric conditions such as ulcers, gastritis, inflammatory bowel disease, diarrhea, and gastroesophageal reflux disease.

7. SMALL INTESTINE

It is associated with blood circulation and hormonal balance throughout the body. The emotions linked to the small intestine are joy, agitation, or feeling lost.

8. LARGE INTESTINE

Its primary role is to dispel waste from the body through the rectum. It also absorbs vitamins, water, and electrolytes from the indigestible food.

The emotions connected to the large intestine are similar to the lungs, including sadness and grief. An imbalance in the large intestine due to your feelings can cause hemorrhoids, irritable bowel disorder, and gastrointestinal diseases.

As you can see, your emotions and bodily organs are connected. Failure to control your feelings can be overwhelming to the body and make you sick. Learning to control your emotions will help keep you healthy. I recommend some form of meditation for 20 minutes a day, twice a day if possible. This helps to calm your mind and your emotions.

Make a choice to be happy. Wake up every day and be grateful to be alive and breathing. Be happy where you are. Only you control your happiness. Don't let your feelings and emotions control you. Don't let anyone steal your joy!

You Can Increase Your Energy

We have already scientifically proven that the Equilibrex® Pendant balances your body's energy by just wearing it. Scientific literature points to three ingredients that are contributing factors to energy, or lack of energy: Exercise, Nutrition, and Thoughts (or attitude).

Science defines energy as the capacity for doing work. Energy can be stored, which is potential energy, and the energy involved in the production of work is kinetic energy.

Humans are dependent on food for energy, and that energy can be transformed from one form to another. This is done in accord with the law of conservation of energy, which states that in the conversion of energy from one form to another, energy is neither created nor destroyed. The energy in food is chemical energy, and it is converted into mechanical and heat energy by the muscles in movement and work.

We know that each food nutrient has a specific role to play in maintaining our energy level. Digested food particles are absorbed into the body's two major transport systems. Fat soluble substances pass into the lymphatic system – which is a network of vessels draining fluid from tissues and later returning it to the bloodstream. Water soluble substances – such as some vitamins, simple sugars and digested protein—are absorbed directly into the blood circulatory system. First they are carried to the liver.

From the liver, the food particles are distributed to each and every cell by the blood circulatory system – which can be called the body's plumbing system. The heart is responsible for pumping approximately nine to ten pints of blood around the complete circuit once every minute, and to every cell in the body when you are at rest.

When the cells get the food particles, the proteins and fats are used to build, maintain, and repair tissues; cells such as those of the skin, blood, and intestinal wall are continually dying off and must be replaced. Most particles of digestion are used to provide energy. This is the most important use of carbohydrates. Cells burn up complex materials in the presence of oxygen to produce chemical energy and form carbon dioxide and water as waste products.

This process is similar to the combustion of gasoline and air in a car engine to produce mechanical energy with carbon monoxide and oxides of nitrogen as wastes.

The real source of energy is the mitochondria. The mitochondria is a minute cytoplasmic structure, known as " the power house of the cell," and is found in every cell.   Potential energy is stored in the mitochondria as glycogen, fat globules and protein. It is released in the form of the chemical adenosine triphosphate (ATP) when it reacts with oxygen.

Oxygen is transported from the lungs to tissues by the red blood cells.   As we inhale, fresh oxygen is drawn into our lungs. As we exhale, circulating blood in the lung   walls, releases carbon dioxide and in exchange, picks up the oxygen.

Cells use up their energy reserves in a variety of ways just to maintain life and carry out their specific roles – muscle cells to contract and nerve cells to transmit impulses, and for growth, repair, and reproduction.

Muscles are attached to bones and convert chemical energy into mechanical energy. With over 650 skeletal muscles in the body, a sufficient amount of food must be eaten to perform any actions.   A well-balanced supply of nutrients is needed daily. If your work involves prolonged physical activity, you may need to eat twice as much as a sedentary worker.

Trouble comes in when a lot of people eat more than their bodies need for nourishment and energy, resulting in obesity and being overweight. Being overweight has a direct effect on your level of energy. For most people, the best way to get an energy boost is to eat less. Food is our main source of energy, but too much is our main source of fatigue. Most overweight people know from experience with dieting – losing and regaining pounds – that there's an inverse relationship between weight and energy. After a certain point, the heavier you are the less energetic you feel.

If you're overweight it's more of an effort to move around. Ordinary activities cost you more in energy. People who are too heavy are generally less active than their thinner colleagues.

Energy also comes from self-confidence, self-esteem, and the thoughts you have about yourself. Heavy people often lack confidence and esteem. It's difficult to feel good about yourself when you're a heavy-weight trapped in a culture that disapproves of being fat and actually discriminates against those who are fat.

Studies indicate that the obese have higher base levels of insulin, and their bodies also release more insulin in response to a meal. This is important because not only is insulin the hormone that removes excess sugar from the blood for storage as glycogen or as fat, but the effects of insulin can also make you feel lethargic and sleepy.

An insulin abnormality is not the cause of obesity. It seems to be the other way around. Getting fat distorts the insulin system.

Once you begin to put on weight, you're caught in a vicious circle. You feel low in energy because of the insulin problem, it's more of an effort to get around, and you're not pleased with yourself so you become less active. The less active you are, the fewer calories you burn, and the fatter you become. Obesity is a self-perpetuating disease, and most diets amount to nothing more than a ride on a seesaw. A person loses weight only to regain it as soon as he or she goes to "normal" eating. You CAN do something about those extra pounds.

Here are the basics of how to lose weight and increase energy. First, we must recognize that the human being is in effect a "heat exchange engine." It must follow the laws that govern energy exchange.

Here is the equation explaining energy exchange and the process of metabolism:

Caloric Balance = Calories Taken In − Calories Expended

Different foods have varying caloric content. We expend calories in three ways:

1. In basal metabolism, which is the rate we burn energy

2. In work metabolism, which is the increased rate of energy expenditure when we are exercising or doing any physical activity

3. Some calories are lost in the excreta.

If an individual takes in more calories than he or she expends, they have a positive energy balance. This is an energy excess. The law of energy conservation tells us, energy can neither be gained nor lost, it can only be changed in form. So what happens to the excess energy? It is changed into body fat. An individual would gain approximately one pound of fat for every 3,500 excess calories.

If an individual expends more energy than he/she takes in, a negative caloric balance will result. They will burn fat (converted energy) in order to make up for the deficit. This fat loss occurs at the rate of approximately one pound of fat for every 3,500 extra calories spent. Therefore a negative caloric balance is what we need to achieve fat loss.

There are three ways to reduce weight:

1. Increased energy expenditure with constant food intake

2. Decreased food intake and constant energy expenditure

3. A combination of 1 and 2

The first method can be accomplished by exercise programs, the second by diet, and the third by a combination of exercise and diet, which is the best.

People who exercise regularly and vigorously have more energy on the days they exercise than on the days they don't. Muscle function can be improved by exercise at any age. In the absence of disease, the improvement is greatest in persons with poorer strength levels at the start. If you've had a negative attitude about exercise, would like to see a negative energy balance (fat loss), would like to increase your energy, start today by making some changes in your lifestyle. Make some change in the foods you eat, maybe eat less, and exercise more.

Change your thoughts and your attitude! When your thoughts are negative, you have less energy. You feel drained and tired. Energy follows thought. When you have positive thoughts of love, health, and joy, you feel full of energy and aliveness.

Take at look at your life. In order to change your energy level, you must change your thoughts and attitudes. You are responsible for your life, and only you can change your energy for the better. With more energy and balance of your energy, your life will take on a new meaning!

GEMS AND STONES

I have studied the power of gems and stones for many years. All the energy can be enhanced by placing the Equilibrex® Pendant next to it. I've done numerous experiments and found this to be true. The electromagnetic energy of the sunlight has been absorbed by the rocks while they were being formed. This energy is present in all gemstones and may be absorbed into our own biological system. Some gemstones make us feel good, if we are sensitive to their vibrations.

As far back as the Bible, gemstones were mentioned and worn particularly in the Old Testament and Book of Revelation. A lot has been written about the identification of these stones, but it mentions that there were twelve sacred stones, as there are twelve astrological signs with their own birthstone. The high priest of the Israelites, wore a sacred breastplate known as "Aaron's Breastplate" with these twelve stones. They were arranged in four rows with three gemstones in each row.

Gem power and gem therapy has been handed down through the ages and many were used for healing different ailments. In ancient Egypt, this was depicted in hieroglyphics and drawn on papyrus. The gems were heart shaped and shaped as eyes. Many were uncovered in the tombs, and they were inlaid in shields, amulets, goblets, and armors. Many eastern civilizations of China, Tibet, and Northern India, felt that the spiritual properties of gemstones were important, plus they had medicinal and protective values. They would wear necklaces with different gems and rocks for protection and guidance. Today many health practitioners use gems and stones for health balancing issues. They can place different gems on your 7 chakras (energy centers in your body), to keep your energy flowing for the best health.

There are so many stones that have been identified, with each given its own powers. Some uses are healing, protection, sleep, stress relief, dieting, increasing brain activity, fertility, balance, and many more powers.

My favorites are Aquamarine. Lapis Lazuli, Sugilite, Alexandrite, Tourmaline, Amethyst, Diamond, Ruby, Sapphire, Emerald, Peridot, and Quartz. All of these gems have been used for experiments and research for centuries. I wear many of them with my

Equilibrex® Pendant to maximize their effect on my energy balance, especially around negativity. You can research each stone, and see what is written about them. The best test is to try each gem on your own, and see how you feel just touching them or wearing them.

Do You Think Like A Winner?

A lmost everything you read concerning health and fitness mentions the importance of positive thinking to achieve success.

Many people attribute their gains to lack of negative thoughts and envisioning their results. I believe one's mental attitude and thoughts are what determine the difference between winning and losing. Exactly how important are your thoughts?

The answer to this question may seem obvious to most of us, but the effects of negative thoughts may not be so apparent.

They are like extra pounds of fat that we are carrying around which can be taxing on us both physically and mentally.

Energy follows thought. Every achievement you experience began as a single thought consisting of a few micro milliwatts of energy flowing through your brain. That thought was followed by millions more. Clocked at 1,200 words per minute, thoughts have a tremendous impact on the mind, emotions, and body.

When negative thoughts arise (which the body perceives as a threat), an automatic physiological response is triggered called the "fight or flight" mechanism. The body reacts as if there is a danger or a threat and prepares to either take action toward the threat (fight), or flee for its life (flight). This was a valuable human response if you were in real serious danger, but it is counterproductive in our daily activities.

The repeated and unnecessary triggering of this response causes the body to produce emergency chemicals (which includes the flow of adrenaline), and if unused, these chemicals eventually begin breaking down into other, more toxic substances. The body must then mobilize yet again to get rid of the poisons, which creates enormous physiological stress. As you can see, this downward mind/body spiral can continue almost indefinitely. When it has gone on for a while, we call it depression. Life is stressful enough, so who needs the extra weight of a negative thought?

Through our many experiments, we have found that when a person is having a negative thought, they can hold on to an Equilibrex® Pendant, and the effects of that thought will lessen. The energy balance of the body regains equilibrium.

CAUSES OF NEGATIVE FEELINGS

- **Intimidation.** Don't be concerned with others. Focus only on yourself and your goals. Thinking and feeling positively about your aims and success will help.

- **Being overly sensitive.** Develop emotional resilience, and don't let outside stimuli get you down.

- **Preoccupation with personal hostilities.** See things as enjoyable challenges. If anger arises, refocus your attention on the purpose of what you are doing. This is also a good time to hold on to an Equilibrex® Pendant.

- **Lack of Control.** Observe negative thoughts as they happen, the incident that triggered them, and how you reacted. Take deep breaths and visualize the thoughts leaving your mind.

- **Self-tormenting internal dialogue.** Feelings of unworthiness result from thoughts such as "I'm not good enough," or "I can't do it, so why even try?" Stop the self-doubts.

- **Unrealistic expectations.** There are no magic pills or potions. Your goals may take a certain amount of time depending on individual factors.

- **Mental Poisoning.** Negative comments, complaining, visual suggestions, and gossip may negatively influence thoughts just by being in close proximity to this behavior. Negative thoughts create negative people, which can hurt themselves and others.

How To Eliminate
Negative Thoughts

- Recognize your potential. Assess yourself realistically.

- Define your Purpose.

- Set your goals. Establish short-term goals that are easily attainable and commensurate with your abilities. Approach goals realistically. Begin slowly, and as each goal is reached, make others until you attain your ultimate desired result. Goals shape what you become. Establish a definite time frame during which you intend to reach each goal.

- Discipline yourself. Think and feel positive about your aims and success. Visualize and feel that you are already there.

- Instill motivation.

- Have self-confidence. Believe in yourself.

- Avoid emotionally toxic people and situations.

- Replace negative thoughts with positive ones.

- Accept things for the way they are. Acceptance is not the same as liking, being happy about, or even condoning a situation. It is seeing something the way it is.

Everything necessary to achieve positive thoughts is within us. Negative thinking is the only thing that can obstruct your goals. Your thoughts create your reality. Motivation, drive and powerful positive thoughts will transform your life from mediocrity to excellence.

THOUGHTS ARE ENERGY AND HAVE A VIBRATIONAL FREQUENCY

E verything in the universe is made up of energy and has a vibrational frequency. Thoughts have a frequency and they are magnetic so they attract like things on that frequency. Like thoughts attract like things. Thoughts are things. This is of major importance because our thoughts create our lives. They can either empower us or limit us.

For centuries much has been written about the Law of Attraction and creating abundance using visualization techniques. When your energy is in balance, you can master everything you want in your life. The Equilibrex® Pendant has helped thousands of people accomplish this. Just looking at the design for a few minutes can relax your brain.

Researchers have found that people have between 10,000-60,000 thoughts a day, and according to the National Science Foundation of those thoughts, 80% are negative. This means that negative thoughts decrease your vibration which can lead to depression and sickness. Positive thoughts increase your vibrational frequency and attract happiness. The brain is always thinking. Most thoughts are happening whether those thoughts are conscious or unconscious. You must try to be aware of your thoughts, and choose your thoughts carefully so that you can emit the frequency of the life you want to live. If you want to change anything in your life, change the frequency by changing your thoughts. Your thoughts are the primary cause of everything. Everything else you experience in your life is effect, and that includes your feelings.

You have to change the way you look at things and how you react to negative experiences. Take the time to look at the different situations in your life from a different view, and you will be surprised how those things change.

Clearing your mind is important for your mental health. If you feel stuck, try:

• Listen to music

• Do a guided meditation

• Go for a walk or do some form of exercise

• Try some breathing techniques

• Draw or paint something

- Do yoga

- Read a book

- Read positive affirmations

- Talk to a trusted friend

- Find someone to motivate you

- Do what you love

Your thoughts are the electricity that lights your world. You have everything you need to be successful. Just put the fire under you. Act like it's going to happen. The only one that can stop you is you! You can plug a lamp in the wall but without electricity it will not go on. You are that electricity!

You can change your thoughts and change your world. Change the way you think and your life will be better. We create our own reality with our thoughts. Positive thoughts can influence your reality and keep you strong both physically and mentally.

I am writing this from my personal experiences. It's hard to let go of negative thoughts when people lie to you, steal your money, steal your ideas, pretend they care to gain your connections, copy your life, etc., yet these thoughts only hurt you. I have to constantly let go of negativity, and be thankful for the Equilibrex®

invention which was sent to me to help people (and Me). We can't dwell on the past, and must live in the now. Life is too short.

Don't give into helplessness. Believe in your strength.

Pay attention to the things you can control, and other things will improve.

Don't be too hard on yourself. You don't have to do it all at once.   Take your time. Focus on the present and take it one step at a time,

Find what makes you happy.

THE SLEEP CONNECTION
TO GREAT HEALTH

A good night's sleep is vital for every human being to survive in this world filled with stress. When an average person sleeps the suggested eight hours in a night, it means that an average person will sleep about 229,961 hours in their lifetime or one third of their life by the time they reach 70 years old. Scientists are still researching the many things that sleep accomplishes. Sleep is interwoven with every facet of our daily life. It affects health and well-being, moods and behavior, energy and emotions, even one's sanity. Good sleep reduces stress, boosts immune function, can lower blood pressure, and most important improves our brain and heart performance. Not getting enough quality sleep regularly raises the risk of many diseases and mental health disorders. These range from heart disease and stroke to obesity, depression, and possibly dementia.

We need quality sleep so that the body and brain can repair itself. Growth occurs, tissues rebuild, detoxification occurs, protein is assimilated, important energy stores are replaced, and much more. Poor sleep affects mental health by disrupting our circadian rhythm and interfering with our normal sleep stages, thereby throwing our bodies out of balance.

Everyone has a unique sleep/wake cycle that is one of many genetically determined biological processes, just like eye and hair color. This sleep/wake cycle is a circadian rhythm that fluctuates at roughly a 24 hour cycle and is governed by an internal body clock. Researchers have discovered a "rhythm gene" in DNA (deoxyribonucleic acid) that contains the body's code for the necessary amount of sleep each individual requires, as well as sleep length, depth and structure.

Our sleeplessness or alertness is determined by the hormonal secretions that regulate body temperature. Most people normally become sleepy between 7 PM and midnight, a period during which body temperature falls rapidly and people are most alert about six hours after waking, when the body temperature is near its highest. When you go to bed during the downward curve of your body-temperature cycle (as most people do), you sleep until the next upward temperature curve, an average of 7.8 hours.

WHAT HAPPENS DURING SLEEP?

When you're asleep, the kind of electroencephalograph (EEG) waves your brain produces differs from those made when you are awake. In a conscious state, the brain generates very small, fast waves or oscillations. When you sleep, it generates slower and bigger waves, depending on how you are sleeping. The reason is that when you're awake, each nerve cell in your brain fires individually. When you sleep, more of the nerve cells start working together.

You alternate between two completely different types of sleep. One is the type during which you dream, called REM sleep due to the characteristic raped eye movements that occur while you dream. The other is non-REM or non-dreaming sleep.

Sleep begins with non-REM, which has four distinct stages or levels:

STAGE 1 ~ LIGHT SLEEP

• Muscles relax and your thoughts drift

- Brain waves slow down from about average waking speed of 13 to 35 cycles (pulsations) per second (beta waves) to 8 to 12 cycles per second (alpha waves).

- Blood pressure drops

- Pulse rate declines by about 10 beats per minute

- Blood sugar and calcium levels rise

- Temperature declines

- The body begins to detoxify, excreting toxins from the cells. This process usually peaks near 4 AM

- You can be awakened easily

STAGE 2 ~ MEDIUM SLEEP

- Brain waves slow to three to seven pulsations per second (theta waves)

- Blood pressure, body temperature, and pulse continue to decline

- Eyes may move slowly from side to side

- You can still be awakened easily

STAGE 3 AND STAGE 4 ~ DEEP SLEEP
MOST IMPORTANT FOR ATHLETES

- Long, slow brain waves of less than four cycles per second (delta waves)

- Muscles are relaxed and breathing is even

- Growth hormone is released by the pituitary gland during deep sleep, which occurs 60 to 90 minutes after sleep begins.

- Body recovery takes place and most of your blood is directed to the muscles. Although the brain is capable of thought during delta sleep, thinking during these stages is sparse and fragmented, due to the diminished flow of blood to the brain

- Tissues are repaired and the immune system is maintained

- 90%of the kidney's function of waste - product is accomplished during this stage

- You are not easily awakened

Stages 3 and 4 of the non-REM period may last from only a few minutes to up to an hour, depending on age, with 25% of total sleep time occurring during young adulthood – more for children and less for older people. You may be described as "dead to the world" in stage 4.

STAGE 5 ~ REM SLEEP, OR DREAM SLEEP

• Characterized by rapid eye movements

• Dreaming occurs

• Brain waves quicken to the speed of 13 to 35 cycles per second

• Your heartbeat and blood pressure fluctuate, becoming irregular

• Breathing becomes faster

• You are in a state of arousal and the adrenal glands pour larger amounts of hormones into the body

• More blood flows into the brain and less goes into the body

Your first nightly encounter with REM sleep lasts from five to ten minutes. This complete trip through the five sleep stages lasts about 90 minutes and then stages two through five repeat themselves with variations in length, from four to five times during the course of one night's sleep. Deep sleep becomes briefer in the course of a night or may disappear, while REM sleep becomes progressively longer, marking the last stage of each cycle.

The total amount and quality of sleep you get is of major importance. Dream sleep is important in that it stimulates the desire to work hard, maintains psychological well-being, consolidates and sorts memory and helps brain development and learning.

Deep (Delta) sleep stimulates growth, revitalizes and restores the body and brain, allows the body to fight infections and illness and maintains psychological well-being. Waste products are expelled and energy reserves are rebuilt during deep sleep.

In order to reach deep sleep and dream stage, your sleep must be continuous, not fragmented with awakenings.

We have found in our studies with people with sleep difficulties, just putting an Equilibrex® Pendant next to their head, or on their body while sleeping, they sleep better, and feel better when they wake up.

CREATE OPTIMAL SLEEP CONDITIONS

- Keep a regular sleep schedule. Go to bed and wake up at the same time every day, even on the weekends.

- Establish bedtime rituals. By following a routine every night you are doing an exercise in conditioning that sets up a mental pattern that suggests sleep. For some people, sex is a pre-sleep bedtime activity, and for others, a hot bath helps induce sleep.

- Exercise is one of the best methods to get your body and mind in shape for an efficient night's sleep, as long as you don't do it too late in the evening.

- Allow time to clear your mind and wind down. Don't tackle any problems or discuss controversial subjects. If you can't sleep, get out of bed. Sleep is one aspect of life in which trying harder doesn't help you succeed. Try reading or concentrate on something that doesn't involve muscular movement.

Focus your mind away from worrying about falling asleep, and it will occur naturally. Get into bed only when you are sleepy.

- Go outside every day and get natural sunlight.

- Do not read, watch TV, or eat in bed if you have sleep problems. This will help you associate the bed only with sleeping.

- Avoid nicotine and caffeine. Caffeine products such as coffee, tea, cola drinks, and chocolate products can take 6-8 hours to wear off completely. They are both stimulants.

- Avoid alcohol after 6 PM and altogether if possible. Alcohol produces poor quality sleep characterized by many awakenings, little or no delta sleep and decreased REM sleep.

- Do not use sleeping pills. They can disrupt sleep patterns, cause addictions, mask other problems, and affect the day after. The effectiveness of most sleeping pills drops off after one to two weeks. They should be avoided whenever people are depressed, drink too much, or have breathing problems.

- Do not sleep with your TV, radio, or light on. Even though it may not awaken you, it can deprive you of needed deep sleep for growth and strength.

- Create a great sleeping environment. Keep cell phones away from your head, as well as any electrical devices. Have a comfortable mattress and pillow. Move your clock to the other side of the room.

- The temperature of your bedroom should not be too hot or too cold. Temperatures below 60 and above 75 degrees F were found to disturb sleep in most cases. Be sure the humidity is right for you. If you have allergies, get rid of dust and other pollutants.

- Eat a light dinner about four hours before bedtime. It should consist of a small amount of protein (to prevent nighttime hunger pangs), complex carbohydrates and low amounts of fat. Although a large late-evening meal can make you feel drowsy, it can also disrupt your sleep cycle by keeping your digestive system working overtime. Avoid snacks that cause indigestion or heartburn, such as fatty foods, heavily garlic-flavored or highly spiced foods. If gas disturbs your sleep, avoid beans, cucumbers and other foods that contribute to this malodorous malady. Many people are sensitive to monosodium glutamate (MSG) which can cause many symptoms, including insomnia. If you notice insomnia occurs on nights that you have eaten Chinese food, MSG may be the problem.

• If you sleep poorly and awaken frequently, especially in the second half of the night, try a low-calorie carbohydrate snack before bed to solve the problem.

LIFESTYLE DETERMINES DESTINY

I am referring to the importance of exercise, healthy nutrition, a strong, positive frame of mind, plus all of the other life influences that I have written about in this book.

An imbalanced immune system accelerates the aging process, and this increases with stress. Stress is the gasoline on the fire of aging and sickness. I have written about several ways to control stress. Exercise is one of the most important ways in my opinion. You can release all of your problems while focusing on your breathing and movements.

Exercise is one of the best ways to slow down aging and stay in good health. There is a tremendous amount of evidence to indicate that the proper amount of aerobic (oxygen enhancing) exercise can slow down the symptoms of the aging process and reduce the risk of many health conditions. As we age, our vital lung capacity and our body's ability to handle oxygen decreases dramatically with age.

The word aerobic means "with oxygen." The term aerobic exercise refers to the effect of bringing increased amounts of oxygen into the body by speeding up the entire biological system. This physical activity is effective because it makes our heart and lungs work harder. As we use our muscles, they require increasing amounts of oxygen which is needed to oxidize the primary fuels used by our muscles. As the oxygen demand goes up, the heart must work harder to supply the necessary blood (oxygen) to the muscles. By measuring the work load and pulse beat, the oxygen consumption of the muscles can be calculated. The cardiovascular system is forced to operate at a pulse range that results in an overall conditioning of the entire oxygen-handling function of the body. This is accomplished by bringing the heart rate into a range that causes the heart to be maximally conditioned.

A simple formula for determining the optimum pulse rate may be determined by subtracting your chronological age from 170. This gives the lower target range of the pulse. The upper range is obtained by adding 10 to the lower figure. Now you can buy many types of gadgets that figure this out for you.

Conditioning occurs when the pulse is brought into the target range for a minimum of 12 to 15 minutes every other day. Examples of this vigorous activity are running, aerobic classes, Zumba dance classes, or cycling. Some experts recommend 120-150 minutes of moderate aerobic exercise each week, which would include fast walking, getting on a treadmill, jumping on a small trampoline, and swimming.

The Benefits Of Aerobic Exercise

- Improves cardiovascular health & prevents heart disease

Aerobic exercise is recommended by the American Heart Association and by most doctors to people with, or at risk of heart disease. Exercise strengthens your heart so that it can efficiently pump blood throughout your body. It promotes faster return of the heart to normal after exercise and lowers resting heart rate.

- Lowers blood pressure

Cardiovascular exercise may help manage high blood pressure. High blood pressure puts stress on the blood vessels and heart. Over time this can cause a heart attack or stroke.

- Maintains a healthy weight

Diet and exercise are needed for weight loss, but aerobic exercise alone may be the key to lose weight and keep it off. It pushes you to burn calories for energy. If you burn more calories than you consume, this results in a caloric deficit leading to weight loss.

• Helps regulate blood sugar levels

Regular physical activity helps regulate insulin levels and lower blood sugar. This is important for lowering the risk of Type 2 diabetes. Insulin is necessary for regulating blood sugar. Aerobic exercise can increase insulin sensitivity so that the body needs less insulin to control blood sugar levels. While exercising, the muscles use glucose from the blood. This helps prevent blood sugar levels from rising too high.

• Reduces chronic pain

Low-impact activities such as swimming or aqua aerobics may help with muscle function and endurance.

• Aids sleep

Individuals with sleep issues seem to sleep better if they had a regular exercise program. Do not exercise too close to bedtime. Try to finish at least 3 hours before bedtime.

• Lowers LDL cholesterol up to 15%

• Increases the HDL (high density Lipo-proteins)

These are the molecules of fat and proteins in the blood that appear to exert a protective effect against heart disease and high blood pressure.

- Increases resistance to all forms of stress

- Increases overall energy

- Reduces the risk of some cancers. These include:

    - Colon

    - Stomach

    - Esophageal

    - Breast

    - Uterine (endometrial)

    - Bladder

    - Kidney

- Improves bone health

Regular exercise helps prevent bone density loss. Weight bearing exercises such as walking and dancing, and resistance exercises are very good for bone health.

Weight bearing exercise helps build and strengthen muscles.

- Increases the chance of living longer

- Benefits the brain

Scientists have found that the brain begins shrinking at age 30. Aerobic exercise may slow this loss and improve cognitive performance.

- Reduces the risk of dementia

- Reduces symptoms of depression and anxiety disorders

- Puts you in a better mood

- Promotes better balance and agility. This will help prevent falls. Falls lead to broken bones and can create lifelong injuries or disabilities.

- Anyone can afford to do aerobic exercise. You don't need to go to a gym.

Any aerobic exercise is better than no aerobic exercise. Now you can see exercise programs on TV, get videos, or just go outside and walk fast. That makes it affordable too. In addition to these workouts, find other ways to increase your daily activity. Use stairs more often, do more physical work around the house and yard instead of having others do it.

If you have asthma, find exercises with shorter bursts of activity, like tennis or baseball. That way you can take breaks to rest your lungs. Always use an inhaler whenever necessary.

Always warm up and stretch before you begin. I suggest 30 minutes a day, on average, five days a week. If you're new to exercise, start slowly, by doing 10 to 20 minutes every other day, and talk with a medical professional for suggestions.

ANAEROBIC EXERCISE

Anaerobic exercises involve short bursts of physical activity. These are anaerobic because they do not involve an increase in the absorption and transportation of oxygen. During anaerobic exercise, the body breaks down glucose stores in the absence of oxygen, leading to a buildup of lactic acid in the muscles.

Examples include:

• Sprinting

• Weight lifting

• High intensity interval training (HIIT)

The main differences are:

How the body uses stored energy

The intensity of the exercise

The length of time the person is able to maintain the exercise

Aerobic exercises are rhythmic, gentle, and of longer duration. Anaerobic exercises are short bursts of high intensity activity.

Aerobic exercise helps to increase endurance, whereas anaerobic exercise helps increase muscle mass and strength. Both types of exercise are beneficial for the cardiovascular system.

Both exercise types help by:

• Strengthening the heart muscle

• Boosting circulation

• Increasing metabolism

• Aiding weight management

I believe doing both types of exercise is beneficial for your body, mind and spirit. There are classes and videos that incorporate both at the same time. There are great benefits to doing both. Your doctor could make specific recommendations for you. Personal trainers are available if you plan to start any anaerobic training.

PHOTO ALBUM

At the Spinx in front of the great pyramid in Giza, Egypt

*In the king's chamber in the great pyramid
where we spent the night, Giza in Egypt*

With my tour group, Giza in Egypt

In front of the great pyramid in Giza, Egypt

At a tent party in Giza, Egypt

At the Stonehenge, England

Raising funds for cancer as MIT's Miss College Girl of 1999

Black Belt in Tae Kwon Do

After a workout

With a quartz crystal at my Wellness Body Mind Spirit Expo

With Miss Wisconsin at my Wellness Body Mind Spirit Expo

ABOUT THE AUTHOR

Dr. Joanne Flanagan is a world-renown expert in stress analysis and reduction of stress. She wrote the book, "Secrets of Revitalization," plus numerous articles for national magazines on stress, nutrition, exercise, sleep, and electromagnetic pollution by electromagnetic fields (EMF's). She was the forerunner of much of the present day research in many of these areas. Dr. Joanne is an incredibly multifaceted lady who has researched many "out of the box" subjects and has taught about them in seminars and lectures. She is an internationally known speaker, and has traveled extensively around the world researching all things that have an effect on health.

Dr. Joanne began writing poems and stories as a child, and won her first contest at seven years old with a poem she wrote. She was on Fox 6 and received a gift certificate. She won again the next year at eight years old, and decided to keep on writing.

Dr. Joanne earned many degrees beginning with an Associate Degree from M.I.T. (Milwaukee), B.S. and M.S. degrees at the University of Wisconsin-

Whitewater. She received her Ph.D in education and psychology from the University of Wisconsin-Milwaukee, where she taught post-graduate courses in Dealing With Stress, and the Columbia Pacific University. She taught school in the Greenfield School District while working on her Master's & Doctorate Degree. She also taught at the Milwaukee Public Schools. Dr. Joanne received a Lifetime Degree from The American Association Of Nutritional Consultants. She received a Black Belt in Tae Kwon Do while she was teaching school and appeared on many TV shows since at that time there were very few women in that sport. She then opened her own Karate School with a national karate champion, called Fighting Arts System. This was the best form of exercise she could find, plus it taught self defense, self discipline, and respect for others which had become so important. She was a teacher at her own school, and encouraged women and children to learn the sport. She produced many exhibitions at schools and other events.

While in college, she competed in "Miss Future College Girl" and won first prize. She then took up modeling and was featured in TV commercials and a few videos. This wasn't challenging enough at that time and the producers told her to further her education which would be much more important in her future.

While teaching 4th grade in Greenfield, she began researching Pyramid Energy. An all district science fair was coming up, and a girl in her class wanted to do some pyramid experiments. She put up pyramids in the room and placed food and other things in them. Everything dehydrated and nothing spoiled. The girl won first place in the science fair!!! Children enjoyed sitting in the pyramids and it had a calming effect on them. Dr. Joanne began researching this energy and decided to resign from teaching and travel to Egypt to see the real pyramids.

In one year alone Dr. Joanne traveled around the world five times in search of physicians and health practitioners who have developed various therapeutic modalities whose effect was supposedly rejuvenation or slowing down aging.

Each trip included Egypt and the pyramids. She said it felt as though she had been there before (déjà Vu), as did many people that came on each tour. Dr. Joanne produced tours featuring several Pyramid Power book authors and met many officials of the Giza Pyramid area. With a lot of talking about the energy in the King's Chamber, she convinced one of them to allow her and a few researchers to stay in the granite filled chamber (which is in the center) at night, after the tours were over so that she could measure the energy and frequencies. It was amazing! It was hard to explain the balancing effect that she felt, but she later duplicated that with her invention of the Equilibrex® design. Napoleon stayed in the King's Chamber for a night in 1798 and it was said that he came out a different man.

Dr. Joanne enjoyed writing lyrics for songs, which she sold to many singers. She then opened a recording studio with a music producer, called Royal Recording Studio, and they wrote and produced CD's and music videos for several famous artists. She still writes lyrics for people. She represented several bands and got them gigs at many fairs and venues, which led to open a Night Club called the Maze. It became very popular with 800 people on some nights and famous singers such as Alicia Keys performed there. Dr. Joanne again went back to her research and lecturing at different health expos.

Dr. Joanne began producing the Wellness Body Mind Spirit Expos 10 years ago. The aim was to have a one stop event for everything health and wellness. This takes place twice a year with speakers and vendors that are experts in their fields and can help everyone learn new ways to enhance their lives.

She designed and produces the SuperBodies® line of clothing for everyone.

Dr. Joanne is the president and founder of SuperBodies® Inc., an institute that researches the nature of hidden stressors that destroy vitality and cause health problems. Her research led her to design and get a trademark on the Equilibrex® pendant, the first of its kind, which balances the body and protects one from electromagnetic fields (EMF's). This research can be seen on her website.

Visit the author at:

WWW.EQUILIBREX.COM

www.ingramcontent.com/pod-product-compliance
Lightning Source LLC
Chambersburg PA
CBHW051724090426
42738CB00010B/2081